CALIFORNIA

CALIFORNIA

BY
RAY ATKESON
AND
DAVID MUENCH

CALIFORNIA

CONTENTS

Library of Congress Catalog Card Number 72-122036

Copyright® 1970 by

Publisher • Charles H. Belding

Designer • Robert Reynolds

Text • David W. Toll

Printer • Graphic Arts Center

Bindery • Lincoln and Allen

Printed in the United States of America

1713—1784

"No service is too great,
no service is too small
for the love of God
and man."

To the memory of Padre
Junipero Serra, whose
sandaled footprints in
California's dust are its
most enduring monuments,
this volume is respectfully
dedicated.

Right: Statue of Padre Serra
surrounded by brilliant red
Bougainvillea in the garden of
Mission San Juan Capistrano.

Below: Moon climbs in the evening sky over downtown San Diego, viewed from the shores of Coronado.

Right: California State Building housing various museums in Balboa Park, San Diego, California. This graceful structure is considered to be the finest example of Spanish architecture in the United States.

Below: Panorama of San Diego Bay yacht harbor and downtown as seen from Point Lomas residential area.

Right: Colorful spinnakers create a spectacular picture as ocean class sailboats race before a good breeze. Air view over Pacific Ocean near Long Beach.

Below: Orange grove near Redlands. In the distance, winter snows on lofty San Bernardino Mountain. Brightly illuminated fountains decorate El Paseo Mall, Los Angeles Civic Center. In background, county Water and Power building always lighted at night. Ribbons of traffic weave together with the joining of San Bernardino and Long Beach freeways. In the distance, snowcapped ridges of 10,064 ft. Mt. Baldy.

Right: Santa Monica and Harbor freeways interchange bordering downtown Los Angeles skyline. New convention center under construction (left center) on 16.5 acre site. The main exhibit hall will seat 15,000 people for meetings, up to 8,000 for dinner.

12   Ice plant blooms give appearance of mosaic carpet.

CALIFORNIA

July, 1769. His face is gray with pain and exhaustion, and sweat has eroded muddy streaks in the dust powdering his cheeks. His dry lips move ceaselessly in silent prayer as he stumbles and slides down the steep rocky side of the deep ravine. He alternately pulls his mule after him and hangs on to the halter rope for dear life as his feet dislodge small avalanches of loose stones and slip out from under him. At the shadowed bottom of the ravine he rests, wipes his forehead with the dingy cuff of his robe, and waits as his companions follow after him, slipping and cursing, sweating and red-faced, yanking their reluctant animals along. He is a small man, only a few inches more than five feet in height, and fifty-six years old. A leg infection troubles him constantly, yet his eyes are curiously serene as he watches their difficult downhill progress.

At length the small group of leather-jacketed soldiers and Christian neophytes from Loreto labors to the bottom of the ravine and stops in the shade to blow and rest. Outdistanced by the main body of men, they had set out six weeks earlier, traveling north through unexplored wilderness, and they are near exhaustion.

"But what does that matter now?" the small priest had written in his diary the night before. "We no longer feel the hardships of our journey; our hearts are filled with joy as we think of all the dear friends we shall clasp in our arms tomorrow."

They scramble up out of the ravine and stand for a moment on its lip, looking in vain out over the plain toward the sea for a glimpse of the main party. The Bay of San Diego lies within the embrace of a sandy arm extending up its seaward side from the south, and the brushy plain is striped with ravines through which the rains of winter flow down from the upper slopes. A few small hills poke up, but there are few trees except along the streambeds and on the higher elevations. Grapevines grow wild and the Rose of Castile is abundant. Rosemary and sage are commonplace in the sandy gray-brown soil. The Spaniards resume their progress toward the sea and rabbits skitter away at their approach. Antelope herds melt out of sight over the rolling hills.

The men make their way diagonally across the plain to reach shore near the mouth of the bay, and in four hours they are in sight of two ships lying at anchor there. In five they are standing on the sandy shore. Gulls, white against the brilliant blue of the sky, wheel and veer in dimwitted excitement and greet the tired men with shrill, reedy shrieks. A launch bobs toward shore from one of the ships, and the oarsmen direct them northward three miles. The men hurry on, a fluid body, each man alternately hurrying and slowing, like leaves blown along with the wind.

Despite his excitement and exultation, the lame priest is the last to reach the rough camp at the top of the knoll. His fellow missionaries run down the slope to embrace him, all but one who remains behind to complete the lean-to of branches and brush which will serve as a church. "It was a great day of rejoicing and merriment for all," the priest writes in his journal that evening, "because although each one in his respective journey had undergone the same hardships, their meeting through their mutual alleviation from hardship now became the material for mutual accounts of their experiences. And although this sort of consolation appears to be the solace of the miserable, for us it was the source of happiness.

"Thus was our arrival in health and happiness and contentment at the famous and highly desirable

> Port of San Diego
> -Praise Be To God-"

For Fray Junipero Serra, accustomed to seeing in everything the benign hand of God, the occasion may indeed have been wholly joyful. But for the other members of the Holy Expedition the small camp was overhung with dread and the odor of death.

For several years the energetic and ambitious Galvez had pressed for Spanish occupation of the little-known territory north of Baja California. It was territory long claimed for the Spanish crown, but there were other projects in New Spain, a territory extending from Chile to southern Arizona, of more pressing urgency and of better potential for financial return. But now the Russians had established trading posts and otter hunting colonies in the Aleutians, and Galvez used their presence to persuade Carlos III that Spanish claims to Alta California were in jeopardy. Accordingly, an expedition was formed to protect Spanish sovereignty by establishing an outpost at the harbor of Monterey, described more than 150 years earlier by Vizcaino as the best on the Pacific coast. A second settlement was to be established at San Diego. Missionaries were to convert and civilize the native population, and the military was to fortify the country against intrusion and protect the missionaries. Three ships departed the Mexican coast independently, each heavily laden with supplies: the *San Carlos,* the *San Antonio* and the *San Jose.* Two overland contingents traveled separately from Baja California. All elements of the expedition were to come together at San Diego.

The *San Antonio* was the first ship into harbor, but two of the crew had died at sea of scurvy and half of the remaining twenty-six were so badly afflicted they could not leave their hammocks. Eight more died at San Diego. The *San Antonio* had been riding uneasily at anchor for nearly three weeks when the *San Carlos* made port after 110 days at sea. Her crew was so scurvy-ridden that the few sailors still on their feet hadn't the strength to lower the sails or launch a boat. By the time Serra limped so eagerly into camp, only two of the sailors from the *San Carlos* were still alive. The *San Jose* was lost at sea with all hands. Three soldiers had died on the march, and numbers of the Indian neophytes had deserted. Already, with the toehold of empire only tenuously established at San Diego, almost 150 men are dead and many of the survivors are miserable with illness and injury.

The Indians in the vicinity, perhaps thirty-five or forty families, are fascinated with the Spaniards, especially with their clothing. Despite generous offers by the priests, who are anxious to attract the heathen to them, the Indians will not touch the Spaniards' food, probably because of the pitiful condition of so many members of the expedition. Soon enough the Spaniards are trading their extra clothing for the food the Indians can provide.

They can offer fish, game and wild plants and roots, but not the maize, squash or beans grown by the tribes along the Colorado far to the east, since those crops cannot survive the long dry summers without irrigation, and irrigation is unknown.

Portola, Governor of Baja California and comandante of the expedition, orders the *San Antonio* to return to Mexico for supplies, making up a crew of the surviving seamen and a few able-bodied soldiers. The ship sails July 9, and arrives in San Blas three weeks later with nine more dead. Five days after the *San Antonio* weighs anchor, Portola departs with more than sixty men to establish a base at Monterey. Serra and two other priests remain behind to tend the thirty-five invalids with the help of a few servants and muleteers and a guard of eight soldiers. On July 16 he erects a large white cross on the hilltop three miles from the harbor where the *San Carlos* is creaking dolefully at anchor, and sings mass in the brush shelter beneath it. Thus the first mission is established in California.

Portola's expedition plods slowly northward along the coast. He rides at the head of the column, and behind him trail a troop of soldiers, a work-gang of Indians with shovels and axes to clear the trail, four trains of twenty-five mules each, carrying provisions for six months, each with drovers and a guard of soldiers, and then the rearguard troop under the command of Captain Rivera, bringing with them the spare horses and mules. The column moved slowly, sometimes only a few hours a day because of the difficulty of the terrain and the uncertainty of finding water and feed for the animals in the arid land. They press north, rest, press on again over the green-seamed brown hills, always in sight of the foam-edged opal of the sea.

They encounter many Indians; short, brown-skinned people whose villages of hemispherical reed huts are concentrated along the coast and in the river valleys between the mountains and the sea. They welcome the Spaniards, feast and celebrate them, until the Spaniards grow sick of the taste of fish.

There are about 150,000 Indians in California, perhaps a third of them in the narrow coastal strip the Spaniards propose to occupy. So easy is it for these people to provide for themselves in this country that they require and have developed little of the formal social organization that has re-

sulted in complex and interdependent Indian societies elsewhere in North America.

They need nothing from their neighbors except, occasionally, some richer land. For this they will fight, and for revenge against violence and the acts of witchcraft in which they profoundly believe, but their warfare seldom amounts to more than sudden ambushes and brief skirmishes in which the tools of the hunt and of the household are turned briefly to homicide. Only the Mojaves, the agriculturalists along the lower reaches of the Colorado, make tools—clubs —to be used exclusively as weapons.

The social isolation of Indian populations from one another is reflected in the diversity of their languages. Seven basic language stocks are represented in California, and these had been broken into twenty linguistic groups which had been splintered in turn into more than 130 local dialects. As a result, the language of one village is not likely to be understood even in the next, and without a common language and a tradition of co-operation, the Indians are ill-equipped to resist the Spanish intrusion in any concerted way even if they could grasp the implications of the Spanish advance. They dress themselves in bird-feather cloaks at the sight of the travelers, and offer gifts of food and entertainment.

Portola follows the scalloped coast to the barrier imposed by the Santa Lucia Mountains, crosses them under the deep-green canopy of oaks spread across their golden flanks, and drops back down to the sea at Monterey by following the Salinas River. But the great open crescent cannot be reconciled with Vizcaino's glowing description of a perfect natural harbor, and they continue north. After three and a half months of travel their way is blocked by an immense inlet, a vast landlocked harbor. At its mouth they see the Farralones and realize they have come too far. Disgusted, they turn back, and reach San Diego at the end of January, slaughtering their mules for food in the final stages of the march. Many of the soldiers are ill, and everyone has suffered from diarrhea. Portola must be carried on a litter. But no lives are lost.

The men left behind at San Diego have not fared so well. Eighteen more men are dead of scurvy, and one had been killed by Indians. And the *San Antonio* has not returned with supplies. Portola orders forty men to return overland to Baja California for cattle and supplies—and to relieve himself of the burden of feeding them from the dwindling stores. He determines to wait three weeks for the *San Antonio,* and to return to Mexico if she does not appear in that time. Serra objects. If the soldiers cannot secure the country for the king, he can still secure its people for God. If Portola goes, he will stay aboard the *San Carlos* to perform his holy mission. And on the afternoon of the last day of waiting the sails of a packet ship are sighted far out at sea. Four days later the *San Antonio* makes port with a cargo of provisions.

On April 16 the *San Antonio* puts to sea

again, bound this time for Monterey. Portola sets out again by land, this time taking only a small contingent of the strongest of his soldiers, and twenty-six men stay behind at San Diego: two priests, nine soldiers and fifteen Indians. On May 31 the land and sea elements of the expedition are reunited at Monterey where they are met by the local Indians who bring fresh-killed deer and antelope from the hills. Grasslands verge on the sandy shore where whales are sometimes washed ashore, and near the mouth of the Carmel River the reeds grow as high as a man on horseback. Seals caper beyond the surf.

On June 3 Serra and Portola dedicate the settlement site to the Faith and to the king with an accompaniment of bells, musket vollies and a salute of cannon from the *San Antonio.* They build three small buildings and on July 9, a few days more than a year after their arrival in Alta California, the men bound for Mexico, Portola among them, depart in the *San Antonio.*

Spanish California is established in the wilderness: two tiny hamlets 450 miles apart, entirely dependent for survival on sea-borne supplies from Mexico and the good will of the Indians. Galvez, in his official report, does not emphasize the difficulties. "God is with us," he writes, "and . . . it is He who has brought our undertaking to a successful issue."

March, 1806. The ship *Juno,* a month out of Sitka, creeps through the wisps of fog at the entrance to San Francisco Bay and slides with the surging tide in a slow turn to starboard.

"What ship are you?" The hail bounces across the gently slopping swells from a small fortification on the shore.

"The ship *Juno,* Russian, from Sitka!"

There is a moment's silence. "Come about! Drop anchor here near the fortress and send a boat ashore!"

In reponse the Russian sailors begin hauling clumsily at the sail. Their efforts are so slow that when the ship at last loses way, and the anchor is cast into the sea, the ship lies beyond the range of the Spanish cannon. The *Juno's* longboat is lowered over the side, and fifteen or twenty Spanish horsemen gallop furiously to the shore, capes streaming out behind them, and wheel their horses to a dramatic halt at the water's edge. They wait in a nervously shifting cluster as the Russian sailors haul at their oars to bring the boat gliding across the slate-gray surface of the bay. A priest on muleback comes bumping down to join the horsemen at a spleen-bursting trot, his sandaled heels thumping against the mule's ribs with each step.

Lt. Davidov and Dr. Langsdorff clamber out of the boat and walk toward the dismounting horsemen as the boatmen and the crew of the *Juno,* gathered at the rail, watch expectantly. A young Spaniard, wearing a red serape and intricately stitched boots, makes a slight, formal bow and introduces himself in Spanish. Langsdorff replies in Russian. The Spaniard smiles apologetically, makes an elaborate shrug and shakes his head. Langsdorff repeats himself in French. It is not understood. German is no better, nor English, nor Portuguese. At last Langsdorff addresses the priest in Latin, and the priest replies. The conversation proceeds: Dr. Langsdorff to Fray Jose Uria in Latin, and Fr. Uria in Spanish to Don Luis Arguello, First Lieutenant of the Royal Presidio of San Francisco and the son of its temporarily absent comandante.

The *Juno,* Langsdorff explains carefully, is commanded by Lt. Khvostov of the Imperial Russian Navy, and carries the Czar's Plenipotentiary, Nicholas Rezanov, who has only recently returned from a mission of state to Japan and has been visiting the Russian settlements in Alaska. The ship was bound for Monterey where he had planned a formal visit, when bad weather had caused some damage to the *Juno* and had reduced their provisions to the danger point. They had put into San Francisco to make the necessary repairs and, hopefully, to reprovision the vessel. Langsdorff waits impassively as his explanation is relayed to the young commander. Arguello asks why there is but one small ship instead of the two larger ones they had been led to expect, and Langsdorff concocts an answer that satisfies him. Except for the fact of Rezanov's presence aboard the *Juno,* every word of Langsdorff's is a lie.

Arguello scarcely hesitates. He invites Rezanov ashore. Davidov and Langsdorff climb back into the boat and return to the *Juno,* and several of the Spaniards leap back up on their horses and race back to the Presidio. When Rezanov, resplendent in his green court uniform, steps lightly ashore, these men have returned with extra horses.

15

the reluctance of the priests to perform a marriage between the Roman Catholic Concepcion and the Russian Orthodox Rezanov without special permission from the Pope. The loading of the *Juno* is as hurried as the single available skiff will permit, and on May 10 she sails.

As she slips between the red rock cliffs at the mouth of the great bay, slapped heavily by whitecaps and slow to answer her helm, a family of sea lions frolics briefly alongside. The *Juno* reaches the open sea and turns to begin tacking northward along the coast. In her holds are 50 tons of grain, 9½ tons of tallow and butter, two tons of salt. In four weeks she makes landfall off Sitka. Guns are fired from shore in welcome, and a small boat, rowed by men as wasted as skeletons, pushes out from shore. In Rezanov's dispatch case is the plan for establishment of a Russian agricultural colony on the California coast to the north of San Francisco. He has seen the wilderness gentled, and he covets its fruitfulness.

November, 1841. They came tumbling down out of the mountains on foot and on horseback, thirty men and a woman with a child, ragged, exhausted, hurrying, strung out in a line four miles long. At a pond near the edge of the broad valley one of the men kills a coyote. So famished are these people that by the time the last man comes up, there are only a few guts left, and he devours them eagerly. He is a young man, big, a Missourian named John Bidwell, and like the rest he is near the end of his rope.

There had been sixty-nine in the party when they had set out from the Missouri River six months before to attempt the first overland immigration of American settlers into California. Though they had less than $100 in cash between them, they were well-outfitted with animals, wagons and supplies. They had read the letters of a former Missourian named Marsh describing the rich, untenanted lands of California, and listened to a trapper named Roubideaux talk of the healthfulness of the place.

They had traveled across country to the Platte in company with a party of missionaries and trappers bound for the Flathead country of the Rocky Mountains, and followed the Platte toward its western headwaters. They saw the Cheyenne, and herds of buffalo so incredibly vast that they galloped past their camp at full stampede for an entire night. Hail the size of turkey eggs fell to a depth of four inches on the plain, and waterspouts, willowy towers of wind-whipped moisture sucked up from the surface of the Platte, had bounced and danced across their trail. They had followed the Sweetwater to the foot of the Wind River Range, and crossed the Rockies at South Pass. They had forded the Green and camped to rest on the Bear. There the trappers and missionaries had turned north toward Fort Hall and the Snake. Half the immigrants went with them, abandoning their plan to reach California. Five of the prospective settlers were already dead or

turned back leaving thirty-two to press on west. All they knew was that California lay somewhere beyond the horizon.

They reached the Salt Lake in September, circled around it and kept on. In the desert they began to fear the approach of winter, so they abandoned the wagons, packing what they could carry on their animals and their own backs. Half the party was walking now, and the best packers took the lead, outdistancing the men who were forced to fuss and tinker with their packs.

They reached the Humboldt River and followed it downstream until it pooled and vanished in a broad tule marsh within an amphitheatre of gray sand and sagebrush. They could often see antelope browsing on distant hills, but could seldom steal close enough for a shot. They began slaughtering their oxen.

Traveling south and west they crossed the Carson and Walker Rivers, following the latter to where it emerged from a massive mountain range rising steeply up from the desert floor. Now very worried about their dwindling provisions and the imminent winter snows, they had no choice but to hurry on. They pressed up into the pine forests, keeping to the course of the river nearly to the summit, tugging and coaxing their animals along with the greatest difficulty.

Beyond the summit they struck a small westward-flowing stream which they followed downhill with increasing difficulty. After several days, they found themselves stranded on a narrow promontory between two sheer-walled gorges. John Bidwell and Jimmy Johns took horses and scouted a way down. At a narrow ledge some distance from where their companions were waiting, the two men argued about calling them along. Johns insisted the trail could be managed, Bidwell that it could not. Johns fired his pistol, signaling the others to follow them, and plunged down the canyonside on a horse Bidwell later described as coming "as near to climbing a tree as any horse I ever knew." Johns made it down, but the rest of the party could not follow. They spent the hours until sundown struggling down to the stream far below on foot and bringing back water for the animals in cups, camp kettles, even their own boots, and prospecting the rocky crevices for sparse handfuls of grass for feed. The following morning they reversed their trail and, eight men to an animal, hauled them back out of the impasse one by one. By the time they found an easier way down they had eaten the last of the cattle. They shot crows to live, and a wildcat. They still had no idea how far ahead of them California lay, nor when the snows would come.

The few animals left to them were starving on their bleeding feet, and the men made meals of rodents as they continued their slow descent of the mountains. Beyond them to the west they could see a purple line of summits on the horizon and supposed that California lay farther still beyond them. Their minds were numb with fatigue and oppressed by the spectres of freezing and starvation. And at last they stagger out onto the broad level plain of the great valley.

After killing and eating the coyote, the party turns north toward a meandering line of trees marking a streambed. There they find wild grapes and kill two sandhill cranes and two antelope. The next day they kill fifteen deer and antelope and jerk the meat for provisions for the climb over the mountain range to the west. They hurry, hunger appeased, but more frightened than ever of the impending winter. Two scouts go out in advance to find the fastest way, and at nightfall only one returns. They have met an Indian on horseback, he says excitedly, and although they could understand nothing of what he said, or nearly nothing, he had worn a cloth jacket. Over and over he had pointed toward the largest of the western mountains and said what seemed to be "Marsh."

In two days the entire party is camped at the Marsh Rancho in the San Joaquin Valley, in the gently swelling foothills of the Coast Range, eating pork and tortillas furnished by their host, and looking wonderingly about them at the California they had traveled so far to reach.

The great central valley had suffered a long summer of severe drought, and the grasses lie dead and gray on the earth, yet there is game everywhere. Antelope, elk and deer number in the tens of thousands and flow across the valley floor in great bands. Nearly as many long-legged, skinny Mexican cattle graze among them. Bears lumber down out of the high country to nibble at the greenery in the tule marshes where, in winter, flocks of ducks and geese cover the ponds almost solidly. Coyotes range everywhere, and mountain lions pad silently down out of the foothills. Swans and sandhill cranes patrol the streams and rivers in which fish flip and flash, and condors hang motionless in the sky, save for a microscopic trembling.

In all of the great San Joaquin Valley there are three ranches, those of Marsh, Livermore and Amador, and one, Sutter's, in the lower Sacramento. Agriculture is limited to vegetable gardens and larger acreages of barley and wheat, all of which are worked by Indians. They plant in furrows scratched by foot-burner plows and sweep the topsoil back over the seed with brooms. When it ripens they harvest it with hand sickles and carry it on the backs to corrals where they spread it evenly on the hard-packed earth floor. They drive a band of half-wild Spanish horses into the corral, haze them into an hour's frantic galloping before setting them free again, and then rake out the threshed wheat. The Indians of the Sierra foothills sortie down to steal horses for food. They and the animal predators take large numbers, but the herds increase.

California is now Mexican territory, and most of the coastal strip from San Diego to Sonoma has been partitioned into large ranchos. The vast mission holdings have been confiscated and sold into private ownership. Some of the missions lie abandoned, slowly going to ruin, while villages have grown up around others. The 30,000 Indian neophytes, deprived of their ancestral lands and their mission lands as well, go into the pueblos to work as menials, or to the ranchos as vaqueros. The great ranchos are as close to self-supporting as the large and industrious Indian labor force can make them. There is little cash in California, and the principal export is still hides and tallow. Trading ships from Boston call at the coastal anchorages to pay a dollar for each folded and tied hide, which have come to be called "California banknotes." The cattle carcasses are left in the interior to rot on the ground.

Government authority is only lightly exercised in California, and the rancheros live like feudal lords. They are generous, proud and improvident. A man traveling in California needs only a blanket and a knife — for these items are in short supply — and he may go where he pleases. There are no hotels or inns in California, and no need for them. Horses are abundant, and a man can take the one he wants simply by grabbing hold of the rope left trailing round its neck. He may ride twenty or thirty or fifty miles to the next rancho and exchange it for another simply for the asking.

John Bidwell is hired by Sutter, a man of preposterous generosity, to dismantle the Russian settlement at Fort Ross, which had been established in 1812 despite the death of Rezanov in Siberia the winter following his departure from San Francisco. Among the materials he transports to Sutter's Fort near the junction of the Sacramento and American rivers is a collection of French muskets believed to have been left behind in Napoleon's retreat from Moscow.

Bidwell's party is the first, but more are coming. In the next year alone there will be 250 American settlers entering California, drawn by the vision of a potential paradise. Among them will be a master carpenter named John Marshall.

July, 1852. The wooden semaphore arm on Telegraph Hill flips upward to signal the arrival of yet another ship carrying adventurers from the east, and yet another vessel slips into the naked forest of varnished spars rising starkly up from the innumerable ships anchored in San Francisco Bay. Small boats scull quickly out from shore to ferry passengers, baggage and cargo ashore at Long Wharf, and when a short, burly man with a broken nose, his two sons behind him, steps out of one of them, a brass band breaks into a thumping "Oh, Susanna!" Tom Maguire, San Francisco's leading impresario and proprietor of the famous Jenny Lind Theatre, leads a swarm of actors, actresses and stage hands to greet the three men, and to lead them along the crowded dock to a waiting carriage.

They clamber in with Maguire and the carriage lurches away from the busy harbor through dusty, windblown streets through which the people — and the rats — of five continents are moving. The ramshackle col-

lection of hovels that sprang up in the glory days of '49 have given way, in the aftermath of fire after disastrous fire, to substantial buildings of brick and dressed stone, even of iron. A steam locomotive chuffs toward them, carrying fill from the sand hills southwest of the city to the rapidly disappearing cove that indents the bay at the foot of Telegraph Hill. Some signs of the haste with which the city was settled still remain: the ships Apollo and Niantic serve as saloon and warehouse respectively, beached on what was once the shore, and is now several blocks from the water. The upper reaches of Telegraph Hill are aflutter with the rag-and-canvas walls of a tent city. But the old sign at Clay and Kearny Streets, "This road is impassable; Not even jackassable," is not needed now, and the famous sidewalk on Jackson Street, built of cast-iron stoves, crates of china, bales of cotton clothing and a grand piano, has been replaced with planed boards. A telegraph line connects with Sacramento, Stockton, Marysville and San Jose, and a plank road is being built out across the dunes to Pipesville, the shanty-town growing up in the vicinity of the Mission Dolores. There are thirty churches in San Francisco and five hundred bar-rooms for a population of just less than fifty thousand cosmopolites.

The Jenny Lind is a large stone building facing Portsmouth Square, next door to the equally-famous El Dorado gambling hall and down the block from the Bella Union, and the sidewalk in front is a roistering crush of humanity even before noon. "I have seen purer liquors, better segars, finer tobacco, truer guns and pistols, larger dirks and Bowie knives, and prettier courtezans here than in any other place I have ever visited," an admiring journalist writes home to his paper. "California can and does furnish the best bad things that are obtainable in America." And for the best of the bad, all of California knows, the region around Portsmouth Square is the capital. Maguire takes the newcomers inside the theatre and shows them the facilities. They are satisfied, even pleasantly surprised, and make arrangements to begin their rehearsals the following morning. The arrival of Junius Brutus Booth, America's leading tragic actor, with his sons Junius, Jr., and Edwin is no small event. His forthcoming presentation of *Richard III* lends a certain ineffable but unmistakable authenticity to San Francisco's exuberant claims to greatness and permanence.

The Booths had set out from New York in the late spring, sailing south to Colon, then slowly west against the gentle current of the Chagres River, poled in flat-bottomed *bungas* by native boatmen who half-sang, half-grunted interminable choruses of "Oh, Susanna!" At Gorgona they had transferred to muleback for the two-day journey across the thickly jungled Isthmus, and at Panama City they had waited among hundreds more California-bound travelers for a ship to carry them north. The church bells of Panama City pealed continuously at the funerals of those who had died of fever, of cholera, of

any number of undiagnosed illnesses before they had even reached California, much less the gold fields. And when a ship did come, there was a ferocious rush to obtain the available space. Because of his fame, perhaps, or his supreme confidence, the elder Booth had managed to secure a cabin after only a brief wait.

Unfortunately for the Booths, the Jenny Lind is sold for use as the San Francisco City Hall, and they must close their performances after only two weeks of playing to an enthusiastic overflow audience. They depart for Sacramento.

Sacramento, a ten-hour steamer trip away, is only a fifth the size of San Francisco, and exhibits little of its glamor. The town stretches back some two dozen blocks from the river toward the empty ruins of Sutter's Fort. Sutter himself is living on the last piece of property remaining to him, his Hock Farm. All the rest has been snatched away by creditors, usurped by squatters and squandered in supporting every restless drifter who comes to him for a grub-stake, a hand-out, a loan or a job. "There is no need for me to go into the mountains to make my gold," he had said in the aftermath of John Marshall's discovery on the American River. "The gold will flow to me."

It had flowed around him instead, though much of it had lodged on his former wheat acreage where Sacramento was growing larger every day despite destructive floods, a raging epidemic of cholera, and the lack of amenities. The streets of Sacramento are churned by a ceaseless procession of wagons carrying freight and provisions to the mines, and by stagecoaches leaving at every hour of the day and night for the mines. There is little glitter to Sacramento; the orchestras in the gambling houses provide what little gaiety and distinction there is to the crude city. And despite the activity at the docks, in the auction houses where merchants bid for the supplies destined for the diggings, in the streets, and at the gigantic horse market at Sixth and K Streets, there is a mood in the air, a certain discouragement blowing down out of the mountains from the mines. Sacramento is falling into a periodic depression, and after a successful opening night at the American Theatre, the Booths play to small audiences. Junius Brutus Booth, as exasperated by the famous and voracious bedbugs of the place as by the indifference of its audience, returns to San Francisco and took ship for the east. Edwin and Junius, Jr., remain and take to touring the diggings.

They climbed out of the pest-hole of the Sacramento Valley into the fat-rumped foothills rising up toward the glaciered peaks of the Sierras like a heap of plump, golden apricots. Had they come earlier, at about the time they arrived at San Francisco, they might have rested for a moment at the crest of a ribby hill between two forks of a small river, in the shade of the pines that take over from the oak trees at higher elevations before descending to the settlement called Indian Bar. A swarm of orange butterflies cloaks the drooping branches of the pine trees like dreamfruit.

Before them, the trail dips down into a deep ravine through which a sparkling stream squirms toward the sluggish rivers of the central valley, and on one of its banks, where the bend of the stream has made a long sandbar, is Indian Bar. The town is a clutter of cabins straggling along a single street, roughly built of mud-chinked logs with mud-and-twig chimneys, a few dozen patched and mildewed canvas tents, and some brush-topped lean-tos built under the pine forest that swoops down the mountainside nearly to the edge of the river. The cabins are the business houses: a bakery, a grocery store or two, a meat market, a blacksmith's shop under an open canvas canopy, a doctor's office, and two or three drinking saloons. There are five hundred towns like this one in the twenty by sixty-mile rectangle in the foothills of the Sierra comprising the Mother Lode, and one hundred thousand miners. At night their campfires make a constellation of dim-flickering stars on the dark mountainsides.

The town is quiet. It is Sunday, and the miners do not work. They are reading, sleeping, mending, gossiping, buying provisions, gambling and getting drunk. A sudden commotion erupts in one of the saloons. There is a hubbub of shouts, screams and curses and the door of one of the cabins bursts open. A tall, husky blond young man pops through the doorway, takes a dozen staggering, hard-pounding steps, and falls forward headlong at the stoop of the bakery. A handful of men crowd into the doorway of the saloon and stare out at him. Others rush up from their tents. "Why, Tom, poor fellow," one of the latter cries wonderingly in the sudden hush, "are you really wounded?"

The man strains, quivering in every muscle and turns suddenly over on his back, banging his head against the bark of the bakery's log wall. His shirt is sopped with blood, and blood is pooling in the cool green grass. Some of the men turn and run into the woods at the sight of him; others rush forward to lift him tenderly into the bakery where there is a narrow table. Another runs for the doctor.

From the open doorway of the saloon a tall man steps carefully out of the shadows. He wears the tight, flared trousers of the Mexicans who are being driven out of the rich diggings by the American miners. A woman clings to his arm, and as the men drift back from their panicked running into the forest, she glares at them defiantly. In this man's free hand is a bloody knife. At first the miners hang back as he promenades threateningly and boldly through the street; then six or eight men make a rush toward him. He is as quick. Leaving the woman and the knife behind, he whirls and dashes for the river, leaps into the current and swims strongly for the other side as it tugs him swiftly downstream. Shots are fired after him in a ragged volley, but he succeeds in reaching the far shore and sprinting to cover be-

hind some rocks. Long before pursuit can be organized he works his way out of rifle range and vanishes down canyon out of the mountains.

Two years ago, even one, this scrape might have been considered a private matter and forgotten in a week. But this is the fourth year of the gold rush, and the mood in the mines has changed. Most of the men have experienced more disappointment than success, and in their frustration they have become less generous about what constitutes acceptable behavior. As the gold they have come to gather becomes less and less accessible and the number of miners continues to increase, the adventure is reduced to hard and increasingly unrewarding labor performed under the most difficult circumstances. Many, perhaps most of the men at the diggings, will spend a season and leave poorer than when they arrived.

The stories of the bonanza finds of the early days still circulate through the camps: the boy who dug a shallow hole and took out 167 ounces of pure gold in two days; the man at Dry Diggings who took out $2000 from beneath his front doorstep; Jenkins, who dug into a gopher hole near Auburn and shoveled up $40,000 before he was done; the Murphy Brothers who took 350 *pounds* of gold out of their claims above Angel's Camp; Bidwell, who struck it rich on the middle fork of the Feather, and Marsh, who dug gold on the Yuba at the rate of $50 an hour and traded with the Indians, one cup of beads for one cup of gold until he ran out of beads, and then sold the shirt off his back for twenty-two ounces more, coming away at last with $40,000. And of the Frenchmen who arrived from Paris with a mining outfit including long-handled rakes with which they planned to fish the larger nuggets out of the streams without getting their feet wet. But there are few men getting rich in the hills around them now.

One English miner speaks for many when he says: "I must have been crazy to come here to eat flour and salt meats, to sleep on the ground, and from morning to night to follow the painful trade of a ditch digger for a little gold. And for that I left my family and friends, interrupted an honorable career, ruined my future in the hope of increasing a modest but adequate fortune. I am well punished." Yet he wipes his bleeding hands on his wet and muddy trousers, tosses his shovel with a splash into the pit he has spent three profitless weeks excavating, and drops down after it to continue digging toward bedrock.

If he is lucky, and can resist the epidemic discouragement, he will find a pocket of dust and nuggets in the stratum of tertiary gravel and clay resting on bedrock. If he is not lucky, the rains will come before he gets to it, and diggings will be impossible. He will leave the mines broke. And if he is unlucky, he will die.

Men are dying in the mines of typhoid and dysentery, from cave-ins and falls, from snakebite, starvation, ptomaine and alcoholism. They get rheumatism from standing

waist-deep in the cold running streams all day long, and ophthalmia from the ever-present dust and the evaporating mercury in the gold recovery process. There are few doctors, and many of them are quacks whose diplomas, if they have them at all, were bought at estate sales.

Yet three-fourths of the men in California list their occupation as "miner" and are quick to respond to the reports of new finds. The Trinity excitement draws thousands who take ship from San Francisco to Trinidad Bay and then hike overland to the mines. One party, outfitting itself with supplies for eight days, takes forty-seven days to reach the diggings on the Trinity River. And when they get there, half mad with hunger, fear of Indian attack and exhaustion, they find the diggings already worked out and abandoned. They have no choice but to walk south for seventeen days, subsisting on rattlesnakes and wild raspberries, reaching Sacramento dead broke. They cannot even afford the $3 fee for one of their party to register at an employment agency offering a dishwashing job.

The day of the goldrusher is waning. Men leave the foothill camps reluctantly to take steady jobs in the cities, or to raise wheat along the rivers in the central valley. More and more, those who remain in the hills have money behind them, money they invest in tunneling or diverting the course of streams and rivers. There are ten such diversions along a single ten-mile stretch of the Yuba, and ninety tunnels in Iowa Hill. At Nevada City a French former sailmaker constructs a hose of canvas with a brass nozzle and experiments with washing the gold-bearing gravel and sand from ancient streambeds down out of the hillsides so that laborious digging is not required. Mining is becoming an industry, and the camps are becoming cities or dwindling to ghosts. Marysville, at the junction of the Feather and Yuba Rivers, has a population of 4,500; Placerville 5,600; Grass Valley 3,000, and Sacramento 7,000. Despite the remaining miners in their small settlements in the foothills, northern California is distinctly urban in character.

And in the largest of the new California cities, a Commission is holding hearings to determine the validity of the Spanish and Mexican land grant holdings of the Californios. Many are disallowed, and even those which are confirmed require tremendous expense on the part of their owners to furnish the required proofs of legitimacy. Yet the ranchos are prospering mightily. With Indian labor the rancheros drive their cattle to San Francisco, Stockton and Sacramento where they bring as much as $350 a head in seasons of short supply, and an average price of $50. There are millions of cattle on the coastal ranchos, representing immense wealth, and the rancheros press their credit to the limit in order to spend magnificently.

The center of this great cattle industry is the forlorn collection of drowsy adobes at Los Angeles. There are barely more than fifty buildings scattered in a loose cluster across the brown plain, few of them more than a single story high. Beer, vinegar and wines are being produced in small quantities, but cattle represent the only significant industry. The heads, hooves and guts of slaughtered animals lie in ghastly heaps at the edge of town, and dogs drag the corruption through the streets. There are 1600 citizens in Los Angeles, many of whom are resentful about the recent ordinance prohibiting the washing of clothes in the fitful flow of the Los Angeles River which is the source of the city's drinking water. A harbor is being constructed at San Pedro, twenty miles away.

El Monte, a small village founded by immigrant farmers from Texas, lies ten or eleven miles to the east, and three ramshackle whisky shops have opened within sight of the Mission San Gabriel, nine miles to the northeast. The land is fertile and rich, and the available water is enough to provide good crops, but California law makes it the responsibility of farmers to fence cattle out of their fields. Still, if voracious cattle are a nuisance, labor is cheap. Behind the Downey Block in Los Angeles is a large corral into which drunken Indians are driven on Sunday afternoons, their earnings consumed in the form of brandy, to be sold as laborers for the week the following morning. Their services bring $2 in cash to the town marshal, and $1 worth of brandy to them at the end of the week.

There are about 50,000 Indians in California now, and a federal grant sets aside 32 acres for their exclusive use as a reservation. 250,000 non-Indians live in California, all but about 8,000 of them in the cities and mining regions of the north. There is little attraction in the south. The mild winters and dry summers draw a few invalids and consumptives, that is all.

April, 1887. He comes by train, piling out of the dirty coach to stand on the crowded platform with his traveling companions of the past five days. They stood there for a moment, tugging their rumpled clothing into something like neatness, some of them shepherding wives and whining children along with them. They are men of some substance, farmers, businessmen, storekeepers, and most of them have come from the middle west with the accumulated capital of half a lifetime to invest in Los Angeles.

Throughout the journey he had listened to their anxious, hopeful speculation about what they would find at the end of their journey, and jotted notes for the article he would write for the *Atlantic*. Over and over again they had swapped favorite passages from the books about California they had studied during their last long winter at home: "The whole of Southern California has a very mild and equable climate," they recited earnestly. "The constant or almost uninterrupted brightness of the skies has, I suspect, a good deal to do with the healthful influences of the climate ... There are no gloomy days."

"... Many treeless plains have ... yielded from fifty to eighty bushels of wheat per

acre, and there is no year in which some adventurous farmer does not discover some new product for which the climate and soil are especially adapted, and which pays better than gold mining." At night, after eating meals they had prepared for themselves on the cast-iron stoves provided for the purpose by the railroad, they bundled up in blankets or slept in their clothes on the narrow wooden cots made by folding down the seat backs in the coaches. Or they pace restlessly through the littered aisles from coach to frowsy coach, wondering if they have done right to give in to their restlessness and come west.

At one of the stations in the desert east of Los Angeles—Needles, perhaps—a Californian boards the train. As they rattle west through the Colorado desert the immigrants squint uneasily out at the barren landscape. When one of them turns to speak to the Californian, the journalist takes down their conversation:

"Anything grow along here?"

"Everything, sir, everything: the most productive soil on God Almighty's earth. All it wants is water."

"Fruits?"

"Fruits? I should say so. Every sort that's known. This country right here is going to beat the world in fruits."

"Melons?"

"Well, yes—no; the fact is, melons don't do so well here. They ain't apt to be good. The vines grow so fast that the melons are bumped along over the ground and bruised."

"Ah?"

"Yes...if you want to pick a melon in this country, you have got to get on horseback."

Now they stand on the railroad platform, hands rubbing uncertainly over stubbled chins and patting surreptitiously at the moneybelts around their waists. They stream out into the dusty street and blink back the bright mid-morning sunlight. The music of a brass band batters the cool, clean air, and leaflets are thrust into their hands. A painted billboard across the street shrieks silently at them: GLADSTONE!

Slowly they disperse, melting into the traffic of the city and moving in every direction. Wagonloads of lumber, brick and stone creak through swarms of lighter hacks and buggies. Another wagon, this one draped with bunting and carrying a brass band as cargo, wheels around the corner and rolls to a stop. Upright poles at each corner support banners reading GLADSTONE! And it is surrounded by people. The journalist is forced by the crush to stop and read the message painted in small letters along the bottom of the banner. "Free excursion to the new metropolis of the Azusa! Four coaches arranged! Departing the Santa Fe at 12:30 sharp! Lot auction! Free lunch! Free band concert!"

With an eccentric flourish the band completes its braying and the musicians take their instruments into the station. More prospective real estate speculators follow them than can squeeze into the waiting coaches. Curious and impressed, the journalist reaches into his pocket and pulls out the printed circular he had received at the railroad station, glancing down at the tiny print as he is jostled by the crowd. "GLADSTONE!" it begins. "...in the midst of the choicest orange groves and vineyards of that delightful section and in the natural center of trade and travel...the most perfect climate in California...all the streets will be graded and water is plentiful and abundant and will be piped to every lot...the First National Bank of Gladstone, which will be built of solid granite. A newspaper will be established at once...A valuable water power furnished from a fall 200 feet high... Hinda Villa Hotel now open...located on two lines of transcontinental railroad, both of which cross lands of the company."

Los Angeles is mad with real estate fever and Gladstone is only one of sixty new townsites platted between the San Bernardino Mountains and sea. The great Los Angeles basin is a pigmy forest of shin-high stakes

aflutter with knotted rags to mark off town lots, streets and avenues in grids across the rolling plain. Along the thirty-six miles of Santa Fe Railway track between the city limits of Los Angeles and the western boundary of San Bernardino County there are twenty-five new cities and towns. There are thirty-six in all in the San Gabriel Valley, and almost as many more, each with extravagant claims to a harbor catering to ceaseless international trade, parade along the curving coastline. In Los Angeles alone, where the population has exploded from barely more than

23

Less than 25,000 descendants of California's Indian population remains.

Among more than a million residents of Los Angeles, 427,348 are church members, and the city ranks ninth in the nation in number of churches. But barely more than half of them are Roman Catholic or orthodox Protestant denominations. There are 204 branches of Aimee Semple McPherson's $1,500,000 Angelus Temple, and despite the scandal of her "kidnapping" in 1926, her church commands the spiritual allegiance of more than 16,000 souls. Almost as many are wearing I AM rings ($12) and poring over the materials contained in their special I AM Decree binders ($1.25), attending services of the Agabeg Occult Church, meetings of the Special Rose Light Circle, rituals of Mankind United, or sessions of the Self-Realization Fellowship of America where plans of a proposed $400,000 Golden Lotus Yoga Dream Hermitage are displayed.

San Francisco newspapers devote pages to the activities of the highly social First Families who own or control the real estate, industries and financial resources of the north. But in Southern California the social elite are not the First Families, who are scarcely known to the general public, but the movie people.

Movies had been made in California since 1908 when Col. William B. Selig finished his *Count of Monte Cristo*, begun in Chicago, on the shoreline at Laguna Beach. A few months later Selig's company built the first film studio in Los Angeles, a board-and-canvas lean-to behind a Chinese laundry on Olive Street, and in 1911 the first Hollywood studio was built by the Nestor Company at the corner of Sunset Boulevard and Gower Street. These early movie makers were the small independents who used bootlegged or pirated equipment in violation of patents issued to Thomas Edison and licensed to a limited number of major companies. They benefitted not only from the high number of sunny days and the variety of available scenery, but also from the proximity of the Mexican border and the haven it provided from process servers. So successful are they that the big companies follow them west. In time they become a major California industry, but their need for expansion capital brings eastern banks and corporations into ownership of the six biggest movie companies. Louis B. Mayer is the highest salaried executive in the United States.

In 1936, thirty-six years after the death of John Bidwell and twenty-five years after the last wild Indian in the United States is captured in a slaughterhouse corral near Oroville, there are more automobile fatalities in Los Angeles than in New York City. Paradise has swollen and taken on hellish and hallucinatory overtones.

On the eve of World War II California has recovered some of its economic strength. Aircraft manufacture is the principal industry of the state and only Detroit produces more assembled automobiles than the plants in California. The migrant families find jobs growing more plentiful in the cities, and are replaced in the fields by laborers from Mexico. When war comes, well-paying jobs are so plentiful that still another migration takes place into California, this one drawing heavily from the south and the southwest. In 1942 alone, 570,000 new citizens come to California to find work in the factories of war.

They build fighter planes and bombers at San Diego and Santa Monica, freighters and tankers at the newly-constructed shipyards on San Francisco Bay. They work in the Portland cement factories, in the state's first steel mills and in the iron mines in the Mojave Desert which supply them. Established industry retools and expands into war production: Yuba Consolidated Gold Fields Limited abandons the manufacture of gold dredging equipment to begin producing howitzers.

On the coast above San Diego 125,000 acres are made into a training facility for the Marine Corps. A huge tract near Monterey becomes the Army's Fort Ord. Navy establishments at San Diego and San Francisco are enlarged and increased. More than ten percent of the American armed forces train in California and a quarter of them make plans to return and settle in the state after their release from service.

At war's end heavy industry is a permanent addition to California's potent arsenal of attractions, and hundreds of thousands of citizens continue the westward flood. In 1962, less than 200 years after Serra had limped into the wretched camp at San Diego, California is the most populous state in the union.

Yet never once since 1848 have as many as half its residents been native-born.

The continuing stream of population into California is said to be the greatest mass migration of individuals in the history of the world. Moving west to California has become an American tradition, and California an eternal alternative—the land of new beginnings.

But because more than half its people have always been the restless and the ambitious, the breakaways and discards of a hundred different and conflicting traditions, there are lumps in the melting pot. California society is an uneasy coalition of strangers whose only shared tradition is a skepticism toward tradition, and it sometimes works awkwardly, as if held together with chewing gum and baling wire. It is no accident that the state which invented motels, supermarkets and gas stations also invented beatniks, hippies and Black Panthers.

California is still the tip of the American arrow. Less and less slowly and more and more surely all of us are wearing California clothing, thinking California thoughts—and facing California problems, and in that sense, California seems to be the ultimate destination for everyone.

No people in the history of mankind have ever lived the way Californians live today, and their way of life seems outlined on the horizon for us all.

Right: Doves excitedly feed on grain around fountain in gardens of Mission San Juan Capistrano. In background is statue of Padre Serra, who founded this Mission on November 1, 1776. It is legendary for swallows to return here each year on St. Joseph's Day.

Below: Waves of ever restless Pacific Ocean roll endlessly against the scenic shoreline of La Jolla.

Right: Lacy lichen drapes itself over stately oak tree in San Ynez Valley northwest of Santa Barbara.

Below: Attractive homes ring Avalon Bay, mecca for boaters, on Santa Catalina Island. Passenger ferry makes frequent trips from the Port of Long Beach.

Right: Fiery ball of the setting sun reflects its blazing color on the gentle shores of Corona del Mar.

Below: Hundreds of pleasure boats find fun in Newport Harbor surrounded by the communities of Newport Beach, Lido Isle, Linda Isle and Balboa Island.

Right: Afternoon sunlight shimmers across the Pacific as sailboaters enjoy their sport off Newport Beach. On Pages 36 and 37 following, playful children trying to capture sea gulls on southern California beach.

Below: Riding the crest of massive breakers offers a real challenge for expert surfers at Huntington Beach.

Right: Early morning fog drifts through a dense grove of graceful eucalyptus trees to form a mystic mood.

Below: Marineland of the Pacific, popular showplace of marine life located on the tip of the Palos Verdes peninsula. This aerial view shows the numerous pools, amphitheaters and revolving observation tower.

Right: Brilliant afternoon sun highlights pleasure boats on the rippled waters of Santa Barbara Harbor.

Below: The towers of Mission Santa Barbara at night. Late afternoon sun silhouettes a cluster of palm trees along Cabrillo Boulevard in Santa Barbara. Nearby, shore birds seek tasty morsels at the edge of the surf.

Right: Afternoon sunlight, rain clouds dramatically illuminate boats moored in Santa Barbara marina.

Below: Sun and fog combined create a spectacular image above Santa Ynez Valley in southern California.

Right: Moreton Bay fig tree roots developed a grotesque pattern in downtown city park, Santa Barbara. This fig tree, a native of Australia, was planted in 1877.

Below: Fog sweeps in along the Big Sur coastline on State Highway I between Carmel and San Luis Obispo.

Right: Highway 1 spans the mouth of Rocky Creek along the spectacular and unspoiled Big Sur coastline.

Below: Headlands and coves form Big Sur country as it sweeps north along the coast for hundreds of miles. A lonesome cypress losing the struggle for survival in a secluded cove—Point Lobos Reserve State Park.

Right: Salmon Creek Falls makes a dramatic drop in the Santa Lucia range, Los Padres National Forest.

Below: Foaming surf washes sands of Carmel River Beach State Park. Pinnacle Rock viewed through arch of Monterey Cypress and fascinating patterns of surf-pounded sandstone in Point Lobos Reserve State Park.

Right: Magnificent hillside homes command spectacular view of surf and coastline near Carmel Highlands. On Pages 52 and 53 following—Offshore winds spin off crests of breakers rushing toward Monterey coast.

Below: Once standing Monterey cypress silhouetted against a colorful sunset on 17 mile drive near Carmel.

Right: Surfbound Pebble Beach Golf Course on the Monterey Peninsula, site of Bing Crosby Tournament.

Below: Giant Pacific breaker seems to explode as it crashes over rock along 17 mile drive north of Carmel.

Right: Spinach under irrigation in the heart of rich Salinas Valley. U.S. Highway 101 traverses this area.

Below: The "Sermon on the Mount" is portrayed in tile on the facade of Stanford University's Memorial Chapel. The thousands of minute pieces each were numbered prior to shipment from Italy for reassembly in this masterpiece at the famous chapel, Palo Alto.

Right: Rare mood of downtown San Francisco and the Bay Bridge captured from Yerba Buena Island as the sun slowly settles toward the Pacific Ocean. The bridge and its approaches stretch for eight miles.

Right: Late evening sun partially silhouettes the campanile of the University of California at Berkeley.

Below: Downtown skyline of Oakland, California, reflected on surface of 155 acre Lake Merritt at dusk.

Right: Huge breakers dominate Point Reyes National sea shore seen from lighthouse north of San Francisco.

Below: The "Great Highway" at the western edge of San Francisco parallels the Pacific for many miles. Still standing as a reminder of past glories of the Panama-Pacific Exposition of 1915, is the restored palace of Fine Arts. Coit Tower high atop Telegraph Hill and sailboat gliding across the water of San Francisco Bay are areas of interest in this famous city.

Right: Brilliantly colored grape foliage marks entrance to Christian Brothers Wine Cellar at St. Helena.

Below: Reconstructed facsimile of Russian Chapel at historic Fort Ross. Mouth of Noyo River offers snug retreat for commercial fishing fleet near Fort Bragg.

Right: Brood mares and their colts graze on rolling pastureland in a northern California inland valley.

70

Right: Autumn's brilliant colors reflected on the Russian River paralleling U.S. Hwy. 101, south of Ukiah.

72

Below: Rugged coastline and offshore rocks dominate the western edge of Patrick's Point State Park.

Right: This well preserved Carson House in Eureka is perhaps one of California's most picturesque homes. It is now a private club for members and their guests.

Below: Spring blooms on native rhododendron in Redwood Creek area of Redwood National Park. Five-finger fern on walls of Fern Canyon. Coastal elk herd appears very docile as it grazes near Prairie Creek.

Right: Spectacular view in Jedediah Smith redwood preserve at northern tip of Redwood National Park.

Below: Cresting wave enveloping offshore rock along Del Norte coastline a few miles south of Crescent City. Memorial lighthouse at Trinidad on northern California coast. Picturesque coastline of Mendocino County.

Right: A brilliant sunset reflects on Pacific breakers along the Del Norte Coastline in northern California.

Below: Autumn foliage and evergreen forests surround rugged granite peaks of Castle Crags State Park.

Right: Burney Creek drops 132 feet over a lava wall in McArthur-Burney Falls State Park off State Hwy. 89.

Below: Mount Shasta (elevation 14,162 feet) seen from U. S. 97 north of Weed near Shasta wilderness.

Right: A duck hunter and his dog head out into the marshland of Tule Lake, California. Large areas of this refuge are open to hunting, situated in the Klamath basin of northern California and southeastern Oregon.

Below: Shasta Dam on the Sacramento River. It impounds 55-mile-long Shasta Lake, offering a wide variety of recreation. Mt. Shasta dominates horizon.

Right: Built of layered lava, Mt. Lassen, largest plug dome volcano in the world, rises to an elevation of 10,457 feet, some 4,500 feet above Manzanita Lake.

Below: A skier glides down a gentle southern slope in Mt. Shasta's ever popular winter recreation area.

Right: Ice melting in midsummer on Lake Helen near 9,000 foot elevation—Lassen Volcanic National Park.

Below: Lassen County's colorful Red Rock Canyon. Foreground, berries hang heavy on hardy juniper tree.

Right: Giant 6,907 foot high cinder cone dwarfs lonesome Jeffrey pine in Lassen Volcanic National Park.

Below: Low hanging clouds offer stark contrast to a dry rice field across the broad Sacramento Valley.

Below: Low hanging clouds offer stark contrast to a dry rice field across the broad Sacramento Valley.

Right: New growth on stalwart sage bush indicates a will to survive in Lava Beds National Monument area.

Below: Graceful symmetry of Capitol dome reflected in nearby pool. Sacramento, once the peaceful domain of Captain John Sutter, is the seat of State Government. Along Interstate 5 one of many rural reflections of the broad, fertile Sacramento Valley and from the air, rice fields form an interesting pattern.

Right: Feather River swirls over boulders on canyon floor at depth of 2,500 feet in lower gorge area.

Below: Mountain retreat in Twin Lakes area near Bridgeport. Looking west at the Sierra Nevada range, a gale force wind is blowing snow high into the sky.

Right: Raymond Meadow Creek follows rocky slope near summit of Ebbetts Pass in Sierra Nevada range. On pages 100 and 101 following—Winter reflection over Sawtooth Ridge and Twin Peaks in the high Sierras casts a brilliant glow on Twin Lake Reservoir. This natural beauty is part of Hoover Wilderness area.

Right: Western yellow pine appears to be winning the struggle for survival over glacial rock along middle fork of Stanislaus River Canyon near Dardanelle.

Below: Quaking aspen and rabbit brush forecast winter's coming to the Sierra Nevada Range eastside. Viewed at edge of Grant Lake on June Lake loop road.

Right: Winter storms prevailed as whitebark pine fought for survival. Green Lake, Mt. Conness (elevation 12,560 feet) and Conness glacier in background.

Right: Middle fork of Stanislaus River cuts through sheer glacial narrows near Dardanelle recreation area.

Below: Lake Sabrina in granite pocket. Distant peaks include Mt. Darwin in Kings Canyon National Park.

Right: Swimmers enjoying the crystal clear waters of Lake Tahoe. In background the Sierra Nevada Range.

Below: A herd of beef cattle grazing on the eastern slope of the Sierra Nevada Range near Bridgeport.

Right: Sugar pine takes shape of an espalier against a mountain wall in the Desolation Valley Wilderness.

Below: Clear waters of Clark Fork of the Stanislaus River pour over granite ledge, Sierra Nevada westside.

Right: Sawtooth Ridge in Twin Lakes area — Sierra Nevada eastside. Foreground, yellow Wyethia plant.

Below: Alpine pasture at the base of Sawtooth Ridge near Bridgeport on U.S. 395—Sierra Navada eastside.

Right: Near the crest of Carson Pass can be seen spectacular reflections of the Sierra Nevada Range.

Below: The Trinity Alps in mid-April. A brilliant California poppy often seen in many areas of the state. Formal plantings in Capital Mall surround the gold domed capitol building in downtown Sacramento.

Right: California's famed Central Valley in early morning. By means of irrigation this rich soil provides a wealth of tomatoes, melons and other produce.

Below: A new section of Interstate 5 sweeps across the 200 foot wide California aqueduct near the San Luis Reservoir. In background, the Delta Mendota Canal, another artery of this huge irrigation system.

Right: Tractor furrowing for irrigation water in Central Valley Reclamation area. Air view near Los Banos.

Below: Golden field of grass offers brilliant contrast to Mt. Tom in background—Sierra Nevada eastside.

Right: An Emerald lake reflects granite peak along middle fork of Bishop Creek—Sierra Nevada eastside.

Below: Old tailing wheels in the Mother Lode mining country along State Highway 49 north of Angels Camp. Tuolumne River flows over a natural granite stairway in Yosemite National Park. Small streams almost without number are found in the Minarets Wilderness area northwest of Bishop on U.S. 395.

Right: Seemingly immovable boulders appear small compared to Half Dome—Yosemite National Park.

Below: Nevada Falls on the Merced River in Yosemite National Park. Lightning creased Jeffrey pine atop Sentinel Dome. Upper Yosemite Falls drops 1,430 ft.

Right: Mt. Conness and Green Lake in the Hoover Wilderness bordering Yosemite National Park. Winds often contort the timberline trees into strange shapes like the fallen, weather-bleached Whitebark pine.

Below: The receding shores of Mono Lake. In background, peaks of Yosemite from left to right: The Koip Crest, Mt. Gibbs and Mt. Dana (elev. 13,050 ft.).

Right: Winter reflections on Merced River ahead of majestic Sentinel Rock in Yosemite National Park.

Below: Upper portion of El Capitan reflected in waters of the Merced River—Yosemite National Park.

Right: Winter's gentle face cloaks Half Dome rising 4,800 feet from the forested floor of Yosemite Valley. On pages 132 and 133 following: Winter sunset on El Capitan above the Merced River in Yosemite Valley.

Right: Morning mist envelops a grove of giants in Sequoia National Park. Bracken ferns cover the earth.